# Bookkeeping Without The Bullsh*t

REBEKAH SCOTT

# Bookkeeping Without The Bullsh*t

WHAT EVERY TRADESPERSON NEEDS
TO KNOW ABOUT TAX & HMRC

REBEKAH SCOTT

Copyright © 2025 by Accurex Accounting Solutions.

All rights reserved. No part of this book may be reproduced or used in any manner without written permission of the copyright owner except for the use of quotations in a book review.

First paperback edition October 2025.

Book designed by Emerald Agency Limited.

978-1-9192048-0-2 (paperback)
978-1-9192048-1-9 (e-book)

Published by Accurex Accounting Solutions.

info@accurexaccounts.co.uk

This book was published in the United Kingdom.

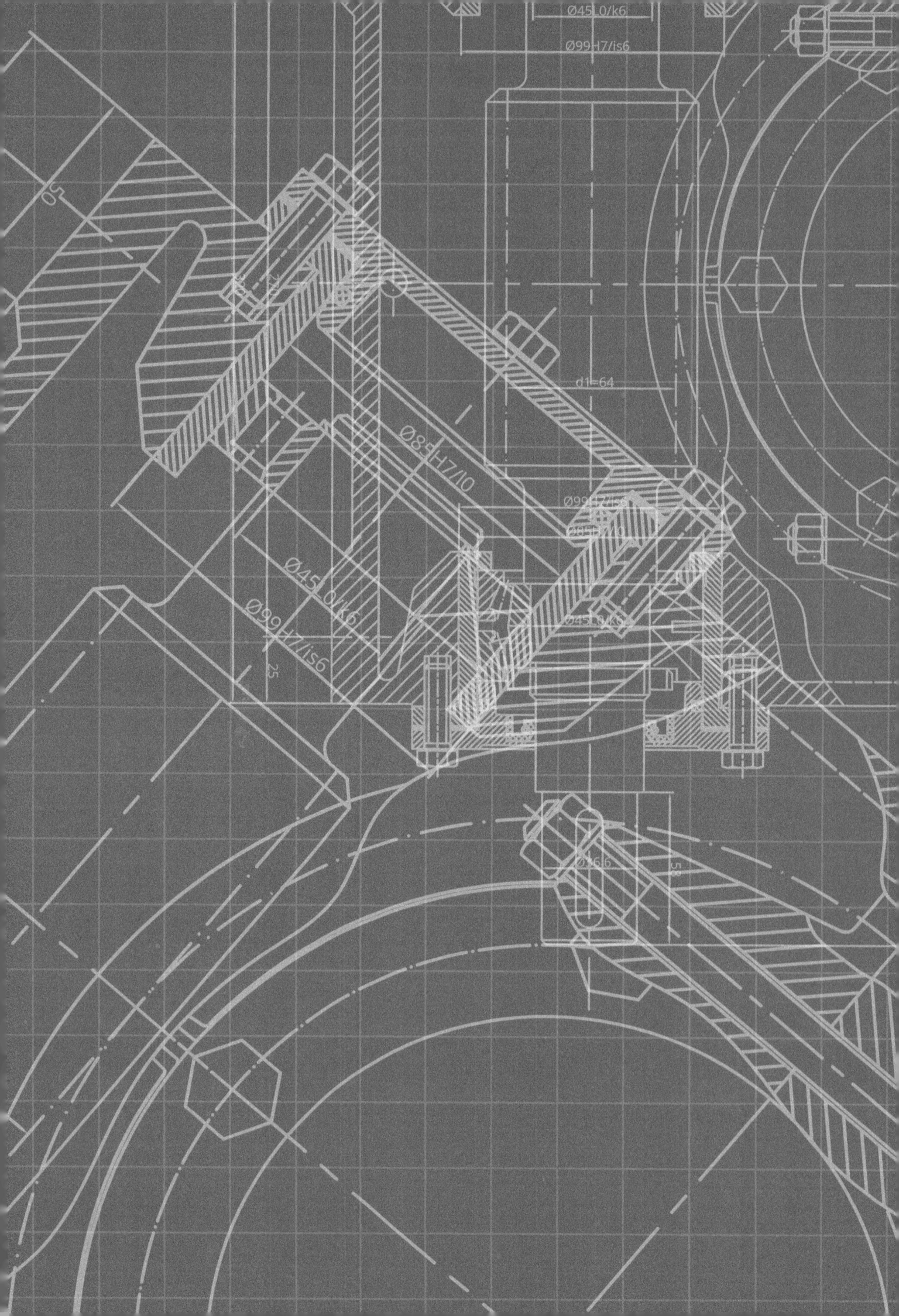

## INTRODUCTION
# Why This Book Exists

Hi, I'm Rebekah — founder of Accurex Accounting Solutions, and I help tradespeople and small business owners get their books in order without the overwhelm, jargon, or eye-watering tax bills.

If you're reading this, chances are you're either running your business full-time or on the tools during the day and trying to keep HMRC happy at night — usually with a pile of receipts, a bit of guesswork, and the hope that it's all "close enough."
This book is for you.

It's not full of fluff, complicated tax rules, or accounting waffle. It's a straight-talking guide to what actually matters when it comes to your bookkeeping and tax — so you can avoid stress, stay out of trouble, and keep more of what you earn.

You'll learn:
- What HMRC expects (and what they don't)
- How to avoid the biggest bookkeeping mistakes
- What you can claim without triggering alarm bells
- Easy systems to stay on top of your finances
- How to make tax time less painful — or even boring (in a good way)

Whether you're a sole trader, just started using software, or you've been winging it for years, this guide will help you make sense of the money side of your business — and give you confidence that you're doing things right.

So grab a brew (or a beer), and let's sort this out together — no bullsh*t.

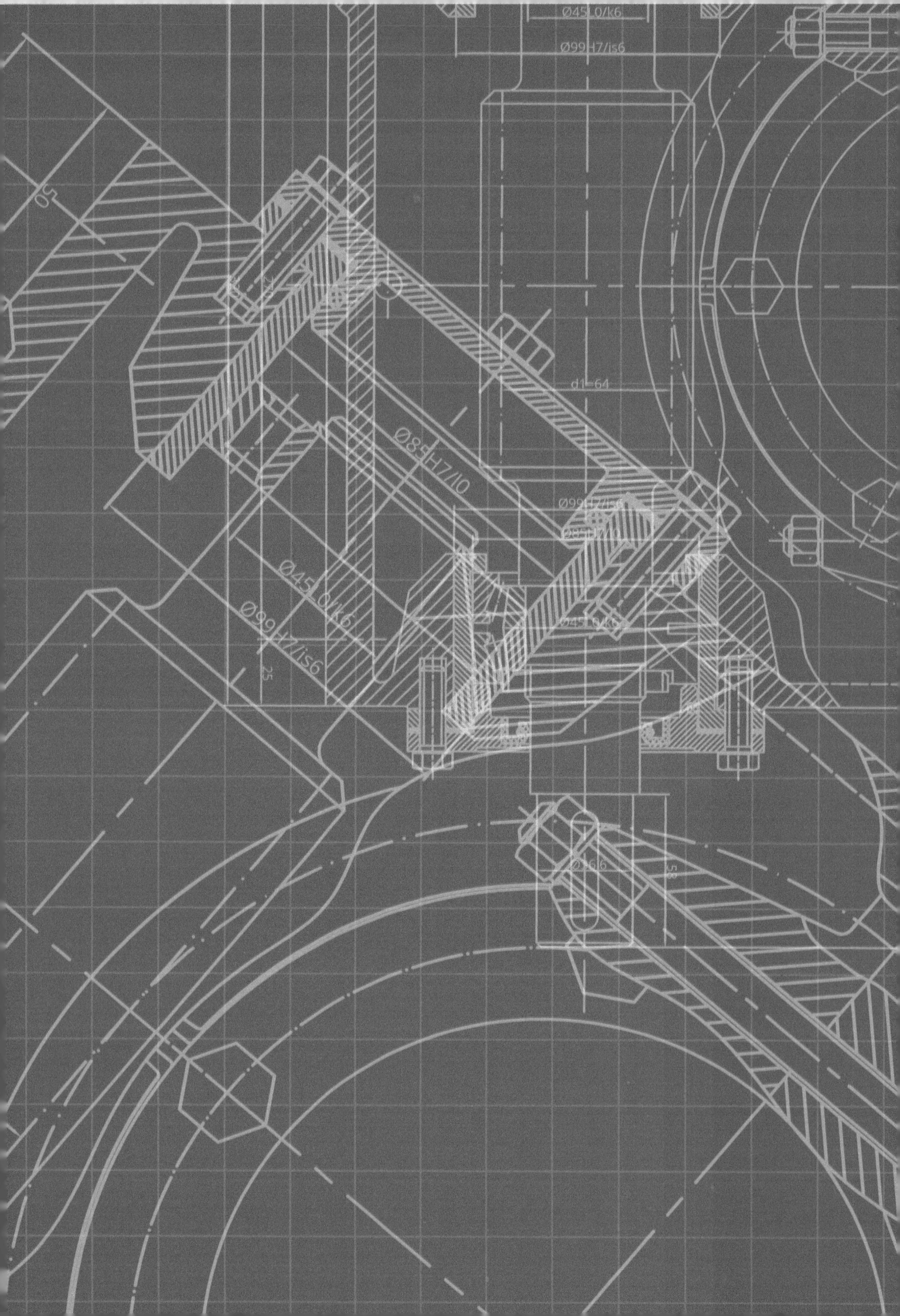

CHAPTER 1

# What HMRC Actually Cares About

Let's be honest — HMRC isn't looking for perfection.

They're not expecting colour-coded spreadsheets or a mountain of paperwork. But they do expect the basics to be done right. That means you need to keep decent records, hit your deadlines, and show your working if they ever come knocking.

In this chapter, we'll break down exactly what HMRC expects — no jargon, no drama, just the facts.

## THE BARE MINIMUM YOU HAVE TO DO

HMRC expects every sole trader or business owner to:

### REGISTER FOR SELF ASSESSMENT
If you're earning over £1,000 from self-employment, you must register. Do it online via gov.uk.

### KEEP ACCURATE RECORDS OF YOUR INCOME AND EXPENSES
That means every job you do and everything you spend for the business — not just bank statements.

### FILE A TAX RETURN EVERY YEAR
Usually due by 31st January if you're filing online. You need to include all your income, even if you've also got a PAYE job.

### PAY YOUR TAX AND NATIONAL INSURANCE ON TIME
The tax you owe is usually due at the same time as your return. If your bill is over £1,000, you may also need to make Payments on Account — we'll come back to that later.

### KEEP YOUR RECORDS FOR AT LEAST 5 YEARS AFTER THE 31ST JANUARY DEADLINE
Yep — even the boring stuff.

If you're VAT registered or running a limited company, you'll have extra requirements

— but this book focuses mainly on sole traders and small partnerships.

## DEADLINES YOU ACTUALLY NEED TO REMEMBER

Here's the no-nonsense version of what you need to know:

| TASK | DEADLINE |
| --- | --- |
| Register as self-employed | 5th October after end of tax year |
| Submit tax return (Self-assessment) | 31st Jan (for online returns). 31st October of the same year (paper returns) |
| Pay tax owed | 31st Jan (and 31st July if you make Payments on Account) |
| Keep records | For 5 years from 31st Jan after the tax year ends |

If you're late, HMRC will fine you — starting with **£100** and rising the longer you leave it. They also charge interest on unpaid tax.

Moral of the story: don't leave it until January 30th.

## WHAT COUNTS AS A "RECORD"?

HMRC doesn't care how you do your bookkeeping — whether it's a spreadsheet, an app like Xero, or handwritten notes. But they do care that:
- Your records are accurate
- You're not making numbers up
- You can back things up if asked

You should be keeping:
- Sales invoices or summaries (what you earned)
- Receipts, invoices, and bank statements (what you spent)
- Mileage logs (if you use your vehicle for work)
- Records of cash payments (in or out)
- Any PAYE or CIS deductions if relevant

The better your records, the easier it is to:
- File your tax return quickly
- Avoid overpaying tax
- Stay calm if HMRC ever asks questions

## WHAT IF YOU GET IT WRONG?

HMRC doesn't expect you to be perfect — but they do expect you to be honest.

If you forget to include something or make a genuine mistake, that's usually OK (as long as you fix it quickly). But if they think you've been **careless**, **deliberately**

**misleading**, or **dodging tax**, the penalties get serious.

Here's a rough breakdown:

| TYPE OF ERROR | PENALTY |
|---|---|
| Honest mistake, told them quickly | No penalty or a small one |
| Careless mistake | Up to 30% of the extra tax due |
| Deliberate, but not hidden | Up to 70% |
| Deliberate and hidden | Up to 100% (yes, double your bill) |

Basically: be upfront, keep your records, and don't take dodgy advice from a mate who "knows someone."

## WHAT THIS ALL MEANS FOR YOU

Here's what you **actually** need to do after reading this chapter:
1. Make sure you're registered with HMRC
2. Know your tax deadlines and put them in your phone
3. Start keeping basic records — even if it's just a folder on your phone
4. Don't panic if you've messed something up — just fix it or get help

You don't need to be an expert — you just need to be organised enough that you could hand things to an accountant without feeling sick. And if the idea of doing all this yourself makes your brain melt, don't worry — the next chapters will show you how to **actually make this manageable** (and when it makes sense to get a bookkeeper like me on board).

## Make It Yours

# Make It Yours

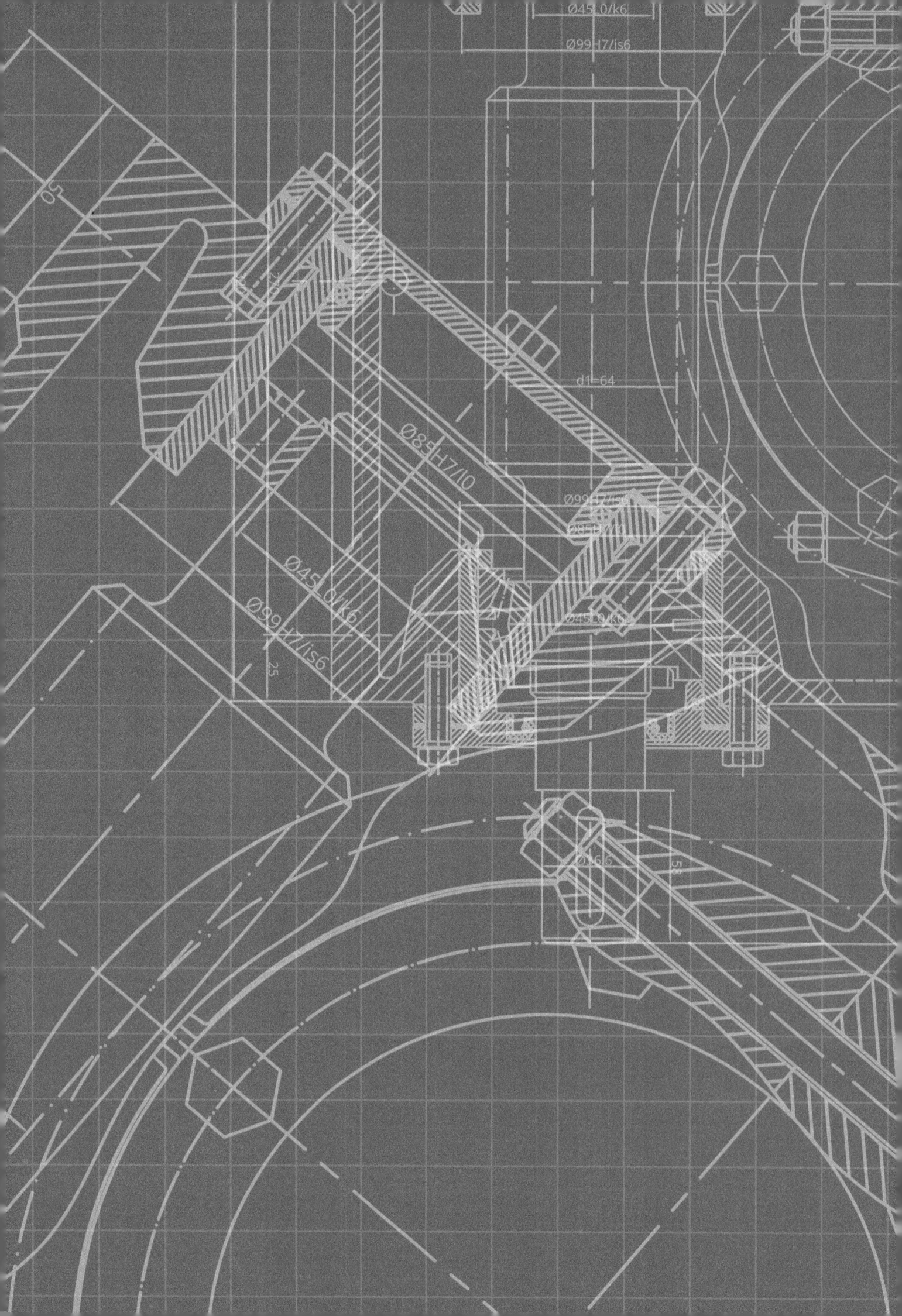

CHAPTER 2

# The 5 Most Common Mistakes Tradespeople Make

*(...and how to stop them costing you time, money, and sleep)*

When I first started working with tradespeople, I noticed the same mistakes cropping up again and again. Not because people were lazy or dodgy — but because no one had ever explained how to do things properly without drowning them in jargon.

These 5 common mistakes can easily trip you up, cost you money, or get you in trouble with HMRC. But the good news? Every single one is fixable — and I'll show you how.

## 1. LEAVING EVERYTHING UNTIL THE LAST MINUTE

You know the drill: it's January 28th, you haven't filed your tax return, and you're scrambling through a pile of crumpled receipts hoping for a miracle.
Sound familiar?

### WHY IT'S A PROBLEM
- Rushing leads to mistakes
- You're more likely to forget things (like expenses you could claim)
- You risk fines or interest if you miss the deadline

### THE FIX
Set a reminder to do your bookkeeping once a week — even just 15–30 minutes. Or outsource it and stop thinking about it completely.

## 2. MIXING PERSONAL AND BUSINESS MONEY

If you're using the same bank account for buying groceries and work tools, it's going to be a nightmare to figure out what's what when tax time comes.

### WHY IT'S A PROBLEM
- Makes it harder to prove what's a business expense
- You'll likely miss tax-deductible costs
- HMRC really doesn't like it

**THE FIX**
Set up a separate bank account just for business income and expenses. Doesn't need to be fancy — just separate. It'll make your life (and your accountant's) so much easier.

## 3. NOT KEEPING RECEIPTS

That £48 tool from Screwfix? The fuel you put in the van? If you haven't kept the receipt or logged the cost, you might not be able to claim it.

**WHY IT'S A PROBLEM**
- You'll miss out on claiming expenses
- HMRC can ask for proof — and if you don't have it, they can reject the claim

**THE FIX**
Start snapping photos of receipts straight away using your phone. Use apps like Xero or Dext to automate it — they're worth every penny.

## 4. NOT CLAIMING WHAT YOU'RE ALLOWED

Lots of tradespeople under-claim because they're scared of doing it wrong. Or they just don't know what's allowed — especially with things like using your home, your van, or your phone.

**WHY IT'S A PROBLEM**
- You end up overpaying tax
- You miss out on legitimate claims you should be making

**THE FIX**
Learn the basics of allowable expenses (we'll cover this in Chapter 3). Or better yet — get a good bookkeeper who knows the ins and outs for your industry.

## 5. TAKING ADVICE FROM THE WRONG PEOPLE

"I just copy what my mate does."
"My uncle said you don't need to declare cash jobs."
"I saw on TikTok that you can claim your whole Netflix subscription."

**Please don't.**

**WHY IT'S A PROBLEM**
- What works for one person might get you in trouble
- Bad advice = penalties, overpaid tax, and stress you don't need

**THE FIX**
Ask someone who actually knows — an accountant or bookkeeper who works with people like you. You wouldn't let a plumber fix your electrics — same thing goes for tax.

## RECAP: STOP MAKING LIFE HARDER THAN IT NEEDS TO BE

If you're guilty of a few of these, don't panic — we've all been there. The goal isn't to be perfect. The goal is to stay organised enough that you're not losing money or sleep over it.

### YOUR 5-MINUTE ACTION PLAN
- Open a separate business bank account
- Set a weekly reminder to review your income/expenses
- Snap every receipt from now on — no excuses
- Ask for help before it becomes an emergency
- Stop taking tax advice from Facebook groups

Next, we'll look at what you're **actually allowed to claim** — and how to stop second-guessing yourself every time you fill up the van, buy a new tool, or work from your kitchen table.

## Make It Yours

# Make It Yours

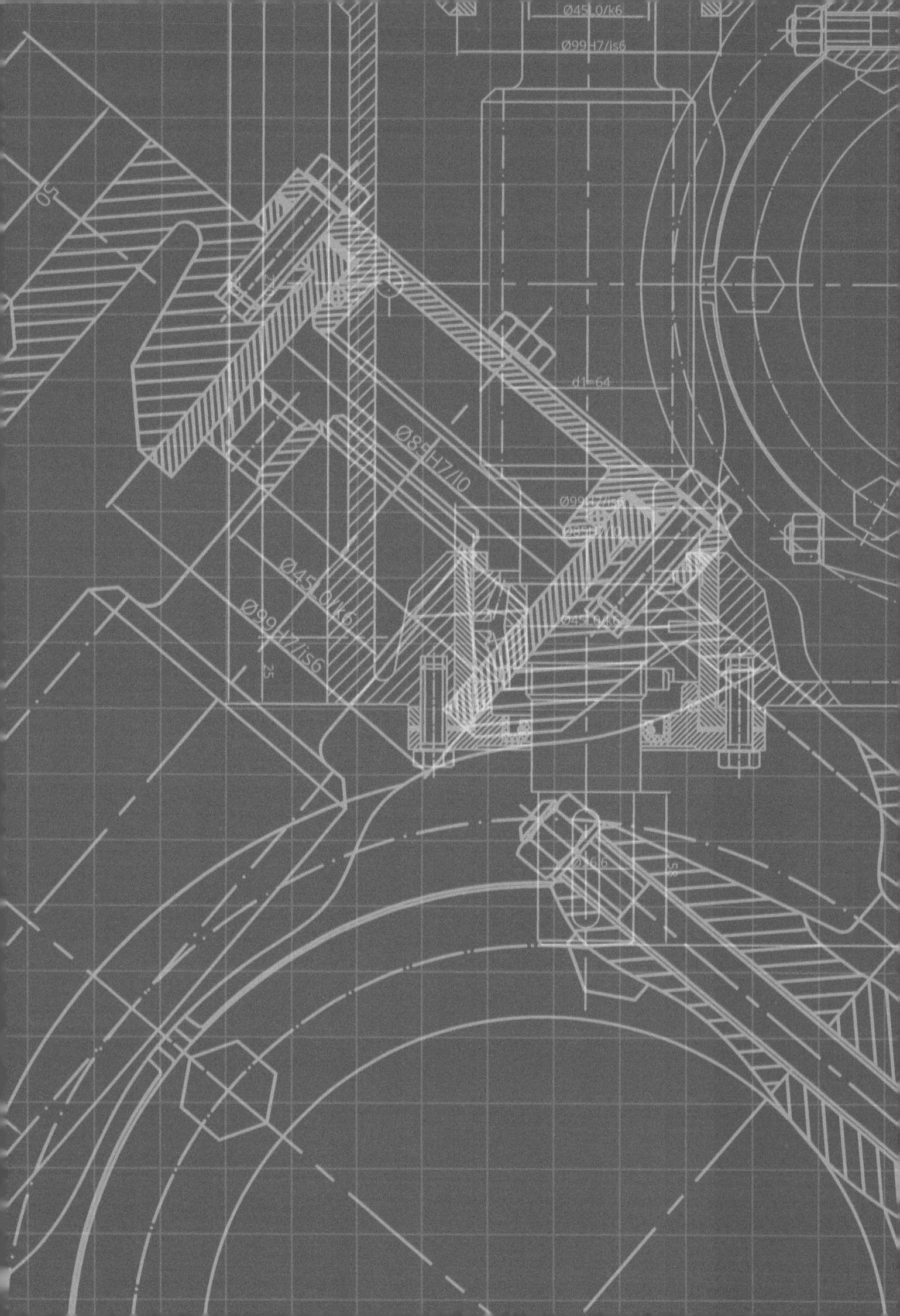

## CHAPTER 3
# What You Can Claim (Without Getting Audited)

This is where most tradespeople either miss out or overdo it.

One guy claims nothing in case he "gets in trouble." The next guys trying to write off his family holiday to Tenerife as "market research." HMRC isn't daft — but they are surprisingly reasonable if you understand what counts.

So let's break it down clearly: what you can claim, what you can't, and how to keep it safe and simple.

## THE GOLDEN RULE OF BUSINESS EXPENSES

If you remember one thing from this chapter, make it this:

"You can claim it if **it's wholly and exclusively for business use**."

That means: if you needed it to run your business, and it's not something you'd have bought otherwise, you're good.

## COMMON EXPENSES YOU CAN CLAIM

Here's a list of typical expenses for trades and motor-related businesses — no guesswork.

### TOOLS & EQUIPMENT
- Power tools, ladders, toolboxes, specialist gear
- Safety gear (boots, gloves, hi-vis, hard hats)

### TRAVEL & VEHICLES
- Fuel for business use
- Van insurance, road tax, servicing
- Parking (NOT fines)
- Mileage (45p/mile for first 10,000 miles if you use your personal car)

**Tip:** If you use your van only for work, you can claim more — but if you also nip to

Tesco in it, the rules are tighter. Keep a mileage log just in case.

### WORKING FROM HOME
- A portion of rent/mortgage interest, heating, electricity, internet
- OR use HMRC's flat rate (£10–£26/month depending on hours worked)

You can't claim 100% of your bills unless you literally live in your van and have no living space.

### PHONE & INTERNET
- Business calls or % of phone contract if it's a mix of personal and business
- Pay-as-you-go top-ups used for work

### INSURANCE & SUBSCRIPTIONS
- Public liability insurance
- Trade association memberships
- Software like Xero, Dext, Joblogic, etc.

### MATERIALS & STOCK
- Raw materials for jobs (bricks, timber, paint, parts etc.)
- Consumables like nails, screws, sandpaper

### MARKETING & ADMIN
- Website, flyers, Facebook ads
- Business cards, logo design
- Stationery and postage

### SUBCONTRACTORS OR STAFF
- Wages, subcontractor payments (must report under CIS if relevant)
- Employer's NI and pension if you have staff

## WHAT YOU CAN'T CLAIM (SORRY)

Even if you're self-employed, there are some things HMRC says a hard no to:
- Clothes you can wear outside work (e.g. jeans or trainers, even if you only wear them on site)
- Lunch and coffee unless you're travelling for work — not your daily Greggs
- Fines, penalties, or speeding tickets (HMRC doesn't reward bad behaviour)
- Gym memberships, Netflix, or your broadband unless there's a clear business reason

**Ask yourself:** Would I have bought this if I wasn't running this business? If not, it's probably claimable.

## WHAT ABOUT DUAL-USE ITEMS?

If something is used partly for business and partly personal (like your mobile phone, van, or home office), you can usually claim a percentage based on use; e.g. If your phone is 70% work, 30% personal — you can claim 70% of the cost.

You don't need to be exact, but you do need to be reasonable — and able to back it up if asked.

## RECEIPTS OR IT DIDN'T HAPPEN

HMRC doesn't require you to keep paper receipts, but you must keep a record — and if they ask for proof, you'd better have it.

Best options:
- Snap receipts on your phone (create a photo album just for them)
- Use software like Dext or AutoEntry to auto-upload and store them
- If it's something like fuel or materials from a regular supplier, log it weekly

You don't need to be perfect — just consistent.

## HANDY CHECKLIST: THINGS MOST PEOPLE FORGET

- Postage costs or delivery fees
- Software subscriptions (Xero, Zoom, etc.)
- Bank fees for your business account
- Training courses (if they're for maintaining your skills)
- Repairs to work van or tools
- Cleaning products used for work (e.g. valeting supplies)
- Protective workwear
- Trade-specific books or magazines

## QUICK MYTH-BUSTERS

**"You can't claim clothes."**
You can if it's protective gear or has your logo on it — but not just jeans or a hoodie.

**"Cash jobs don't count."**
Yes they do. And you must declare them — it's still income.

**"My mate claims his whole Netflix and Spotify as 'business development'."**
HMRC will laugh… then fine you.

## BOTTOM LINE

Most sole traders either:
- Under-claim (and pay too much tax)
- Over-claim (and risk HMRC penalties)

You don't need to be scared of claiming expenses — just be fair, consistent, and keep records. Or hand it off to someone like me who'll make sure you're not missing anything and keep it all above board.

## Make It Yours

## Make It Yours

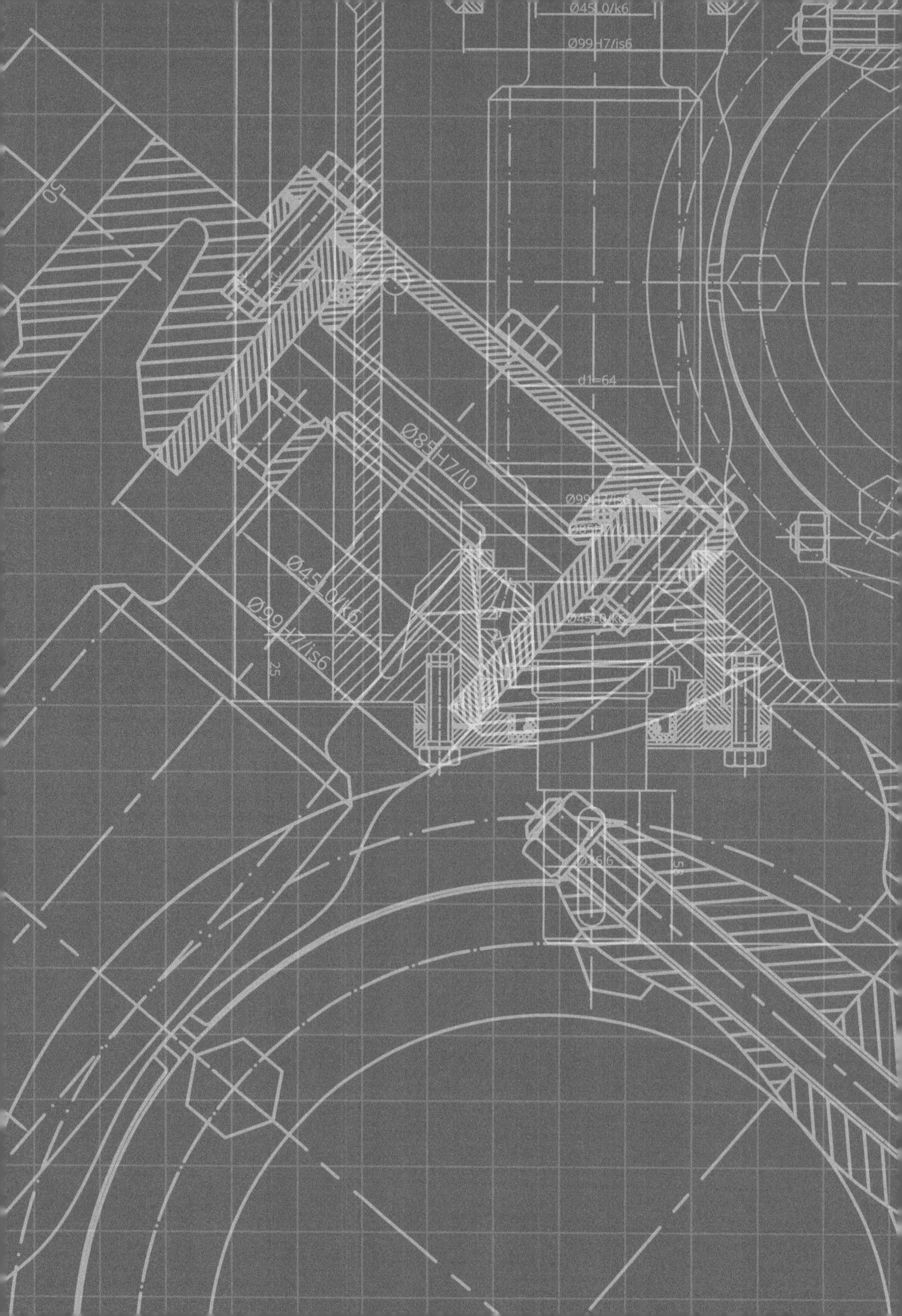

## CHAPTER 4
# Bokkeeping That Doesn't *Drive You Mad*

*(Simple systems that won't take over your life)*

Let's get real — you didn't start your business to spend evenings stressing over spreadsheets or losing weekends to receipts.

The good news? Bookkeeping doesn't have to be a nightmare. In this chapter, I'll show you how to keep things ticking over with a simple system — whether you're using an app like Xero or just starting out with a spreadsheet.

## FIRST: WHAT EVEN IS BOOKKEEPING?

Bookkeeping is just the fancy word for tracking what money comes in and what goes out of your business.

That's it.

Done properly, it helps you:
- Know how much profit you're actually making
- Avoid tax season panic
- Stay out of trouble with HMRC
- Make smarter decisions (like when you can afford new tools or a van upgrade)

### OPTION 1: THE SPREADSHEET SYSTEM
If you're just starting out or doing a small number of jobs a month, a simple spreadsheet can do the job.

Here's what you need to track:
- Date
- Customer or supplier name
- What it was for
- Amount (in or out)
- Category (e.g. fuel, tools, income)
- VAT amount (if registered)

**Do this once a week** — set a 30-minute slot in your diary. That way, it never piles up.

Need a spreadsheet template? I've got one — just ask.

### OPTION 2: USING SOFTWARE (XERO, FREEAGENT, QUICKBOOKS)
Using proper software will save you hours. You can:
- Snap receipts with your phone
- Connect your bank and auto-match payments
- Raise invoices on the go
- Share access with your bookkeeper/accountant

I recommend Xero for trades and motor businesses — it's user-friendly, reliable, and does everything you need.

You don't need to be a tech wizard. Start with the basics: raise invoices, record expenses, reconcile the bank.

## YOUR WEEKLY BOOKKEEPING ROUTINE (15–30 MINS MAX)

Here's what a healthy weekly habit looks like:

### MONDAY MORNING (OR WHATEVER SUITS YOU)
1. Upload any new receipts (photo, email, or app)
2. Enter or review income from completed jobs
3. Reconcile your bank — match payments to invoices/receipts
4. Log any cash payments or mileage
5. Chase unpaid invoices (optional but helpful)

**Tip:** Use one folder in your van or a zip wallet for receipts. End of week? Snap them all, then bin them.

## YOUR MONTHLY BOOKKEEPING ROUTINE (30–60 MINS)

At the end of each month, do a bigger check-in:
1. Review your profit: How much did you make after expenses?
2. Check you've got all receipts for that month
3. File invoices and bills properly
4. Check your tax pot — are you setting enough aside?
5. Send updates to your bookkeeper (or review them yourself)

## SETTING MONEY ASIDE FOR TAX

This is a biggie.

Just because the money is in your account doesn't mean it's all yours. To avoid a tax panic in January, start doing this now:

**Put aside 20%–30% of every payment you receive into a separate "tax pot."**

Most online banks let you create savings pots — or just open a second account and forget the login!

## KEEP IT CLEAN

If you follow these habits, your books will stay in decent shape — and you won't dread tax season.

Your Bookkeeping Golden Rules:
- Don't mix personal and business money
- Don't ignore it for months at a time
- Don't guess — record it properly
- Don't bin receipts until you've logged them
- Don't do it all yourself if it's stressing you out

### WHAT IF YOU'RE ALREADY IN A MESS?
First off — don't panic. I've seen everything from biscuit tins full of receipts to people who haven't filed for years. You're not the worst, and it can be sorted.

If you're behind, focus on:
1. Getting the last tax year up to date
2. Creating a clean system going forward (even if you haven't fixed the past yet)
3. Asking for help — it's not a weakness, it's a smart business move

## BOTTOM LINE

Bookkeeping isn't about being perfect — it's about being consistent.

Do it little and often, use the tools available, and don't be afraid to outsource the bits that slow you down. You'll save time, stress less, and probably even save money in the long run.

## Make It Yours

# Make It Yours

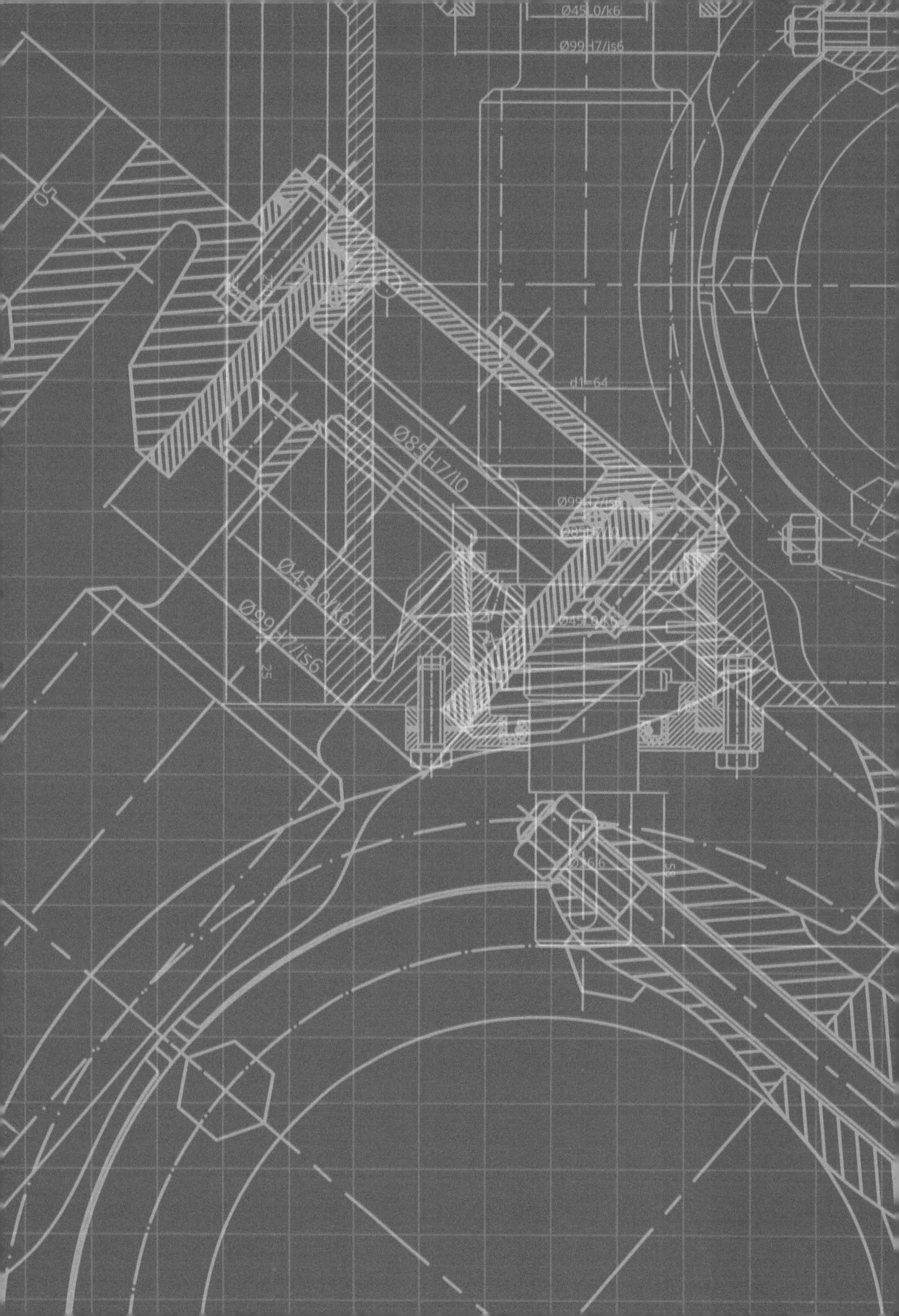

# CHAPTER 5
# How to Handle Cash, Cards & Bank Transfers

*(...without losing track of anything or falling foul of HMRC)*

One of the biggest headaches for tradespeople is dealing with how people pay you. You've got a bit of cash, a few bank transfers, the odd card payment... and suddenly you're not sure how much you've actually earned — or what HMRC will expect you to report.

Let's fix that.

## 1. CASH JOBS — YOU STILL NEED TO DECLARE IT

Let's get the awkward part out the way.

Cash still counts as income.

If you're paid in cash, it must go through your books just like a bank transfer. Not declaring it is tax evasion — and it's just not worth the risk.

HMRC can (and do) check whether your reported income matches your lifestyle. If you're driving a £30k van and claiming you only made £12k... red flags go up.

**WHAT TO DO**
- Record every cash payment (amount, date, job/customer)
- Keep a copy of the invoice or write a receipt
- Pay it into the bank where possible — or clearly track what you used it for (e.g. bought fuel or materials)

You're not expected to be perfect — just honest and consistent.

## 2. BANK TRANSFERS — EASY TO TRACK, EASY TO MISS

Bank transfers are great because they're clear and traceable. But some people forget to match them to invoices — and that's how jobs go unrecorded.

**WHAT TO DO**
- Always issue an invoice for every job
- When the payment hits your account, match it to that invoice (this is called reconciliation)
- If you're using software like Xero, it'll prompt you to do this every week — super easy

**Tip:** Use your business account only for business payments. It makes reconciling fast and simple.

## 3. CARD PAYMENTS — SQUARE, SUMUP, ZETTLE, STRIPE

Card readers are great for professionalism and ease — especially if you don't want to carry loads of cash.

But many people forget about the fees taken by these platforms — and accidentally under-report their income or over-claim expenses.

**WHAT TO DO**
Let's say you charge £100 through SumUp.
- The customer pays £100
- SumUp takes a fee (say £1.50)
- You receive £98.50 in your bank

**IMPORTANT**
You should still record £100 as income, and £1.50 as a fee (business expense).
Not just the £98.50 you received.

## 4. PAYING FOR MATERIALS OR FUEL WITH CASH

Some tradespeople like to use cash from a job to quickly grab materials or fuel without waiting for it to clear into the bank. That's fine — as long as you record it.

**WHAT TO DO**
- Keep the receipt
- Write on it: "Paid in cash from [Job Name]"
- Log it in your bookkeeping system with the job/customer name (I have an excellent system on Xero for this – just ask)

That way, you can still claim the expense and link it to the right income.

## 5. PETTY CASH (IF YOU CARRY A FLOAT)

Some people keep £50–£100 in the van or wallet to cover things like:
- Parking
- Emergency materials
- Topping up fuel

Totally fine — but treat it like a mini bank account. If you use £20 from it, make a note and log what it went towards.

**Think of cash like a bank:** if money comes in or goes out, it should be written down somewhere.

## HANDY CHECKLIST: RECORDING PAYMENTS

| PAYMENT TYPE | RECORD AS | WHAT TO WATCH FOR |
|---|---|---|
| Cash | Income | Must be declared, keep a log or invoice |
| Bank Transfer | Income | Reconcile to invoice |
| Card Reader *SumUp/Square) | Full amount as income + fees as expense | Don't just record net payment |
| Customer Pays for Materials | Still income to you | You may need to show both income and matching expenses |
| You Pay with Cash | Expenses | Snap receipt + note what job it was for |

### WHAT IF IT'S MESSY ALREADY?
Don't worry. If you've been paid in different ways and haven't been tracking properly:
1. Start from today with a clear system
2. Use job sheets, Google Forms, or a simple notes app to log income & costs per job
3. Speak to a bookkeeper to help tidy it up — especially before tax return season

## FINAL WORD: HMRC ARE NOT THE ENEMY

If you make genuine mistakes and you're trying to fix them, HMRC are usually reasonable.

But if you don't declare cash, try to hide income, or make it up as you go — that's when you get into trouble.

A good system isn't about being a goody two-shoes — it's about protecting your business and your peace of mind.

## BOTTOM LINE

You can use any payment method that suits your business — just don't let it turn into chaos.

### KEY HABITS TO STICK TO
- Record every payment, no matter how small
- Snap receipts straight away

- Don't mix personal and business money
- Track fees from card readers
- Reconcile regularly so you always know where you stand

## Make It Yours

## Make It Yours

# Make It Yours

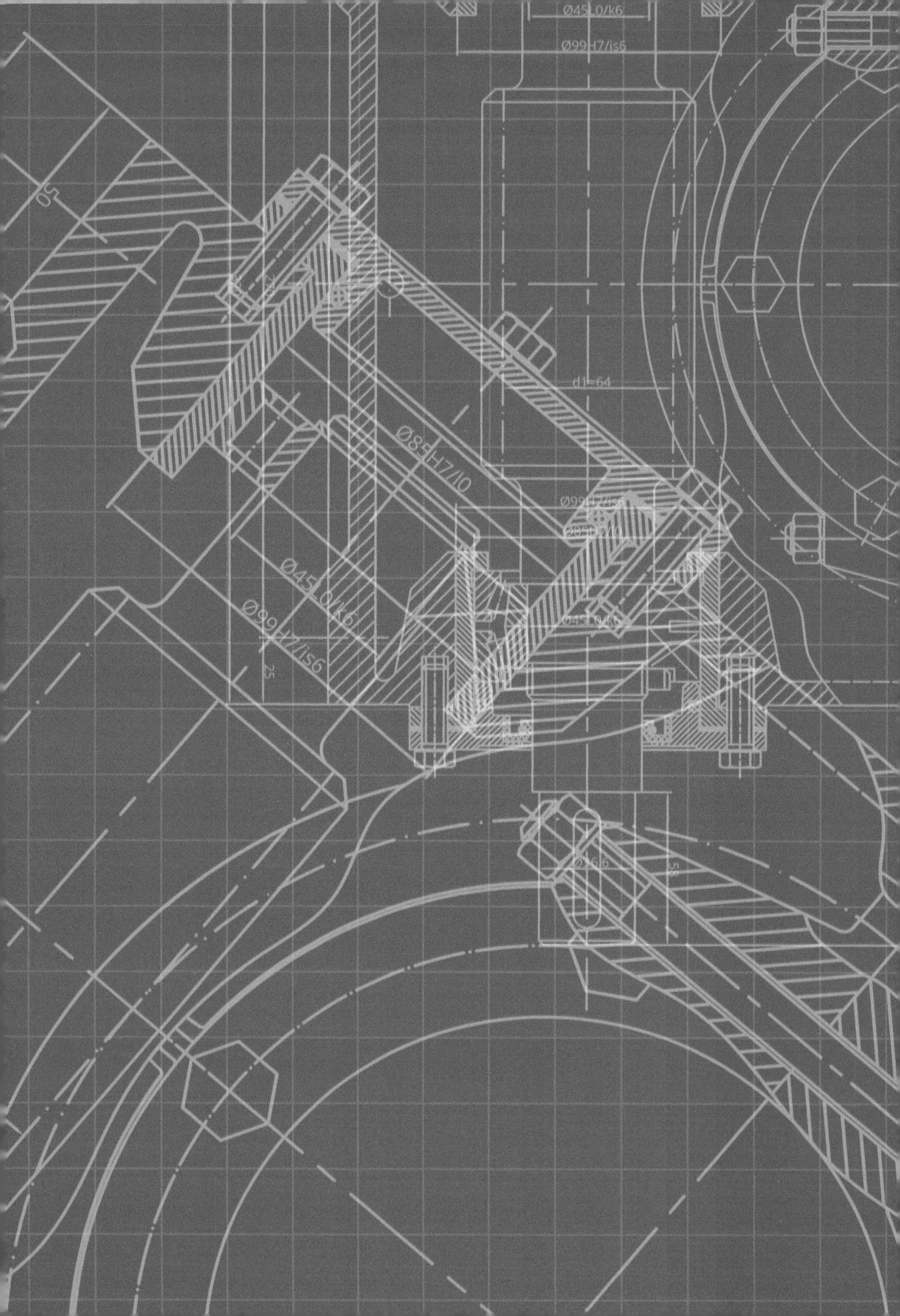

## CHAPTER 6
# What Happens If You Ignore HMRC (and What to do Instead)

Spoiler: It doesn't end well — but it's never too late to fix it

Let's be honest — HMRC letters can make your stomach drop. It's tempting to bury your head in the sand, shove that brown envelope in a drawer, and tell yourself you'll "deal with it later."

But here's the truth:

**Ignoring HMRC always makes things worse.**

Late? Messy? Behind on your returns? You're not the first — and you won't be the last. What matters is what you do next.

## THE REAL RISKS OF DOING NOTHING

If you don't file your tax return or pay what you owe, HMRC doesn't just forget about you. Here's what can happen:

### 1. AUTOMATIC PENALTIES
Miss the deadline? You'll be fined:
- £100 if you're even 1 day late
- Then £10 per day after 3 months (up to £900)
- Then more at 6 months and 12 months

And that's just for not filing. You'll also be charged interest on anything unpaid — and it adds up fast.

### 2. RISK OF INVESTIGATION
If you avoid submitting returns, file random guesses, or don't declare income properly (especially cash jobs), HMRC may launch a compliance check. That's their nice word for an investigation.

They'll ask for:
- Bank statements

- Invoices
- Receipts
- Explanations

And if you can't back things up? They can issue estimated tax bills, fines, or demand repayment of tax credits or refunds.

**3. BAILIFFS & LEGAL ACTION**
This is rare, but it does happen.

If you ignore final demands, debt collectors can get involved. They may:
- Freeze your bank account
- Seize assets
- Set up automatic deductions from your income

Don't panic — this is worst-case stuff. But I've seen it happen, and it's always from burying things for too long.

## BUT WHAT IF I'VE ALREADY MESSED IT UP?

Then here's your get-out-of-jail plan.

**HOW TO SORT IT (STEP-BY-STEP)**
### Step 1: Face It
Find out:
- What years you've missed
- What returns are overdue
- What fines you've already had

You can check this all via your HMRC login — or call them (they will help if you're trying to get back on track).

### Step 2: Gather Your Info
Even if it's messy, you can start piecing it together:
- Bank statements
- Invoices
- Receipts
- A list of customers/jobs per year

You don't need a perfect record — just start with what you have.

### Step 3: Get Help if You Need It
This is where someone like me comes in.

I've worked with people who were 4 years behind, scared stiff, and too embarrassed to speak to HMRC. We cleaned it up, got the returns in, and even had penalties reduced.

HMRC wants you back in the system — not to ruin your life.

They're surprisingly reasonable if you engage.

### Step 4: Make a Plan for the Tax Bill
Can't afford to pay it all at once? You can usually:
- Set up a Time to Pay plan
- Spread the bill over 6–12 months (sometimes more)
- Avoid further action as long as you stick to the agreement

### Step 5: Don't Let It Build Again
Once you're caught up, put a simple system in place going forward. Even if you just send invoices from your phone and snap receipts, that's enough to stay on track.

**PRO TIP: YOU CAN ALSO 'CONFESS' SAFELY**
If you've made genuine mistakes or not declared income, HMRC's Let Property Campaign (for landlords) or Digital Disclosure Service (for sole traders) lets you declare it before they come after you.

It's confidential, you'll usually get lower penalties, and they'll work with you to pay it off.

## WHAT NOT TO DO

- Don't ignore letters
- Don't guess numbers or fudge invoices
- Don't file a return saying "£0" just to avoid the fine — that's fraud
- Don't assume you're too far gone to fix it — you're not

## BOTTOM LINE

HMRC is like a dog with a bone — they won't forget, but they're not out to destroy your business either.

The sooner you face it, the less painful it'll be.

And once it's dealt with, the relief is unreal — you can get back to growing your business, not hiding from letters.

## Make It Yours

## Make It Yours

# CHAPTER 7
# Making Tax Digital (MTD) and *What it Means for You*

*(And how to get ready without a meltdown)*

You might've heard the phrase Making Tax Digital thrown around — usually with a bit of panic, confusion, or a sarcastic eye-roll.

So let's break it down.

This chapter gives you the plain-English version of what MTD actually means, how it affects your business, and what you need to do (hint: it's not as scary as it sounds).

## WHAT IS MAKING TAX DIGITAL (MTD)?

MTD is HMRC's plan to move the UK's tax system online — to reduce errors, make things faster, and get rid of messy old paperwork.

The goal?

All businesses and self-employed people will eventually have to:
- Keep digital records
- Submit quarterly updates using approved software

### WHEN IS THIS HAPPENING?
You might've heard a few dates already — because MTD has been delayed more than once.

Here's the current plan for sole traders and landlords:
### From April 2026
If you earn over £50,000 from self-employment or property:
>You'll have to follow MTD rules from April 2026.

### From April 2027
If you earn over £30,000, but under £50,000:
>Your deadline is April 2027.

### From April 2028
If you earn over £20,000, but under £30,000:
> Your deadline is April 2028.

### Under £20,000?
Not confirmed yet — but MTD will likely become mandatory eventually.

## WHAT DOES THIS MEAN FOR YOU?

If you're self-employed, this is what will change under MTD:

| CURRENT SYSTEM | MTD SYSTEM |
|---|---|
| 1 tax return per year | 4 x quarterly submissions + 1 end-of-year adjustment |
| Can use spreadsheets, paper records, or apps | Must use MTD-compatible software |
| Submit via HMRC portal | Submit through software only |

### WHAT YOU'LL NEED TO DO
### 1. Start using digital bookkeeping
- No more notebooks or scribbled job sheets — you'll need to:
- Track your income and expenses digitally
- Keep records of receipts and invoices
- Reconcile your bank transactions regularly

### 2. Use MTD-approved software
Apps like:
- Xero
- FreeAgent
- QuickBooks
- Sage

All of these are MTD-compliant and will walk you through the submission process. Don't worry — you don't have to file anything quarterly yet, but using software now gets you ready in advance.

## WHY IT'S ACTUALLY A GOOD THING

I know… government schemes rarely feel "helpful."

But MTD can work in your favour:
- Catch issues early — regular updates mean you won't be hit with a surprise tax bill
- Stay more organised — no more lost receipts or late nights in January
- Understand your profits properly — and plan better for growth

And if you already use software like Xero, you're halfway there.

**BUT WHAT IF I'M RUBBISH WITH TECH?**
You're not alone — and the software companies know this.

That's why:
- Most apps are mobile-friendly (snap receipts, raise invoices on your phone)
- There are walkthroughs, support lines, and even bookkeepers who'll manage it for you
- You don't need to become an accountant — just get familiar with the basics

## DON'T WAIT UNTIL IT'S MANDATORY

If you leave it until the last minute:
- You'll be learning under pressure
- You might rush into software that doesn't suit you
- You risk fines if you miss deadlines

Start now, while there's time to get comfortable.

## BOTTOM LINE

MTD is coming — but you've got time to prepare, and it's not as complicated as it sounds.

Start using software, keep things digital, and lean on your accountant or bookkeeper for support. You'll be ahead of the curve, and better off for it.

## Make It Yours

# Make It Yours

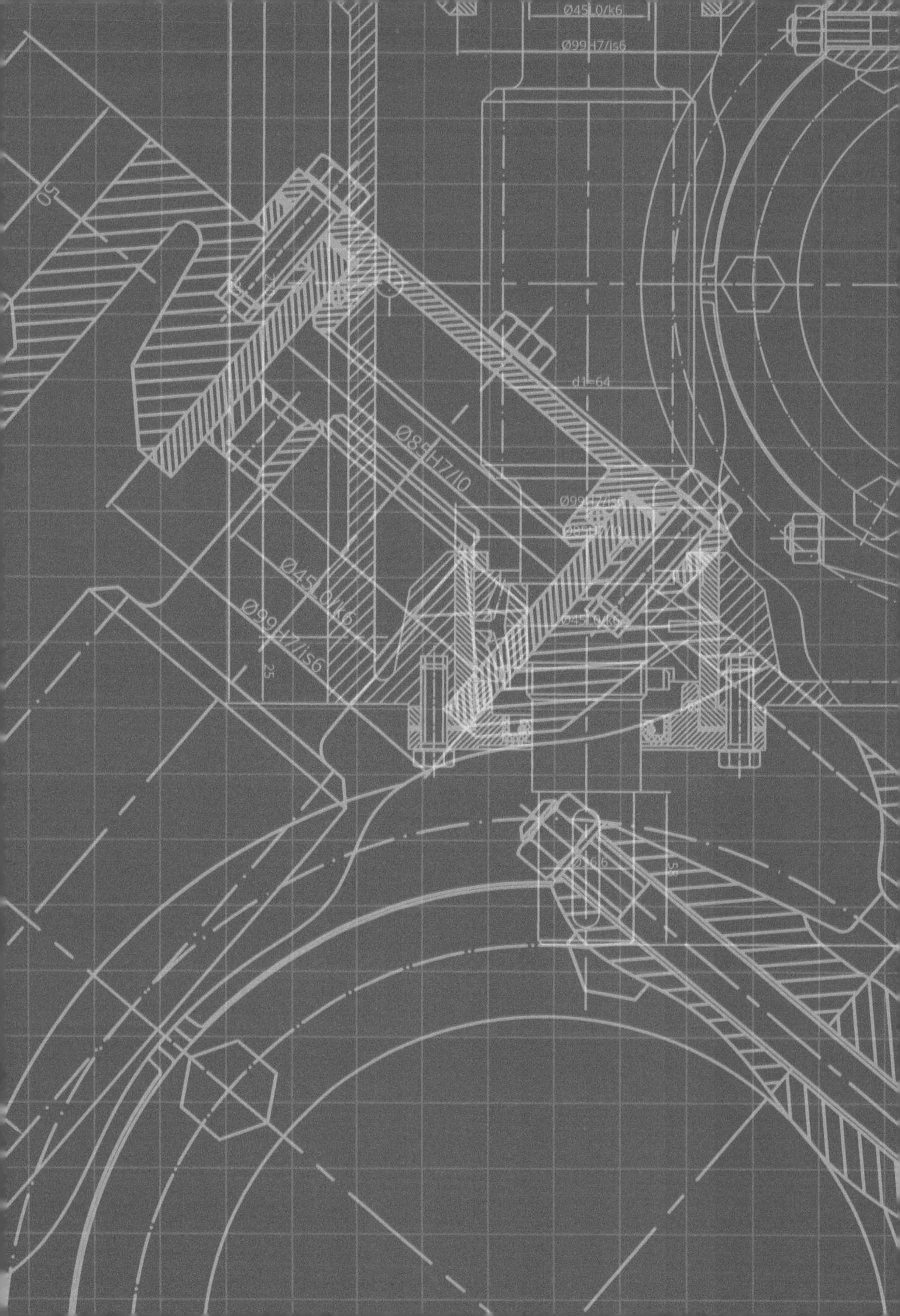

## CHAPTER 8
# How to Pay Yourself Properly

*Whether you're a sole trader or a limited company.*

It's your business. You've grafted for the money.

So naturally, you want to pay yourself — but how?

This chapter breaks down the right way to take money out of your business, avoid tax surprises, and stay on the right side of HMRC.

## FOR SOLE TRADERS

If you're a sole trader, you and the business are legally the same person. That means:
- There's no "wage" or payslip
- You're taxed on profit, not what you withdraw
- You can take out as much as you like — but you need to budget for tax and expenses

### HOW TO PAY YOURSELF
- Transfer money from your business account to your personal account whenever needed
- Call it a "drawings" or "owner's withdrawal"
- Keep a clear record of what you've taken

### BUT HERE'S THE CATCH
You still pay tax on the profit — not what you leave in the account.

So even if you leave £5,000 in the business, if you earned £30,000 in profit for the year, you'll be taxed on the full £30,000.

### Example:
- You bring in £45,000 in income
- You spend £15,000 on business expenses
- Your profit = £30,000

- You withdraw £20,000 to live on

You'll still be taxed on £30,000 — not £20,000 — because that's your profit.

**This is why you need to set aside tax money as you go. (More on this in Chapter 9!)**

## FOR LIMITED COMPANIES

This one's trickier — because a Ltd company is a separate legal entity from you. So you can't just dip into the business bank account whenever you feel like it.

There are 3 main ways to take money out of a limited company:

### 1. SALARY (VIA PAYE)
You become an employee of your company. This means:
- You get a monthly payslip
- The company deducts income tax and National Insurance (and pays employer NI too)
- You must report this via HMRC's PAYE system

Usually set at a low, tax-efficient level (e.g. around £1,047/month in 2025/26)

### 2. DIVIDENDS
Dividends are payments to you as a shareholder, after the company has paid its tax.
- Only paid if the company makes a profit after tax
- You must have company minutes declaring the dividend
- You get a dividend voucher (not just a bank transfer)

More tax-efficient than salary — the first £500 is tax-free (as of 2025).

But can't be paid if the business hasn't made enough profit.

### 3. DIRECTOR'S LOAN ACCOUNT (DLA)
If you take money from the business that isn't salary or dividends, it goes through your DLA.

You can:
- Lend money to the company (and get it back)
- Borrow from the company (but you'll pay tax if it's not repaid quickly)

This is where a lot of directors get caught out. Taking random amounts with no plan can lead to:
- Extra corporation tax
- Benefit-in-kind tax
- Personal tax charges

Always speak to your accountant before borrowing from your limited company. There are ways to do it smartly.

# KEY DIFFERENCES AT A GLANCE

|  | SOLE TRADER | LIMITED COMPANY |
|---|---|---|
| Legal identity | You are the business | Separate legal entity |
| How you get paid | Transfer = drawings | Salary + Dividends (or DLA) |
| Taxed on | Total **profit** | Salary = PAYE; Dividends = after-tax profit |
| Admin needed | Simple | PAYE, dividend paperwork, accounts etc. |
| Flexibility | Very flexible | Needs more planning |

### BIGGEST MISTAKE TO AVOID
"I'll just take money out when I need it and figure it out later."

This is where people get stung.

If you don't:
- Track what you've taken
- Set money aside for tax
- Know whether it's salary or dividends

…then you could accidentally overdraw from the company, miss tax deadlines, or end up with penalties.

### WHAT YOU SHOULD DO
If you're a sole trader:
- Know your profit, and withdraw what you need
- Track drawings properly
- Set aside 20–30% for tax/NIC

If you're a director:
- Plan your salary + dividends with your accountant
- Don't mix personal and business spending
- Keep your records clean (Xero makes this easier!)

## BOTTOM LINE

You can pay yourself however you like — as long as it's done properly.
The more you plan, the more you save (in tax and stress).

## Make It Yours

## Make It Yours

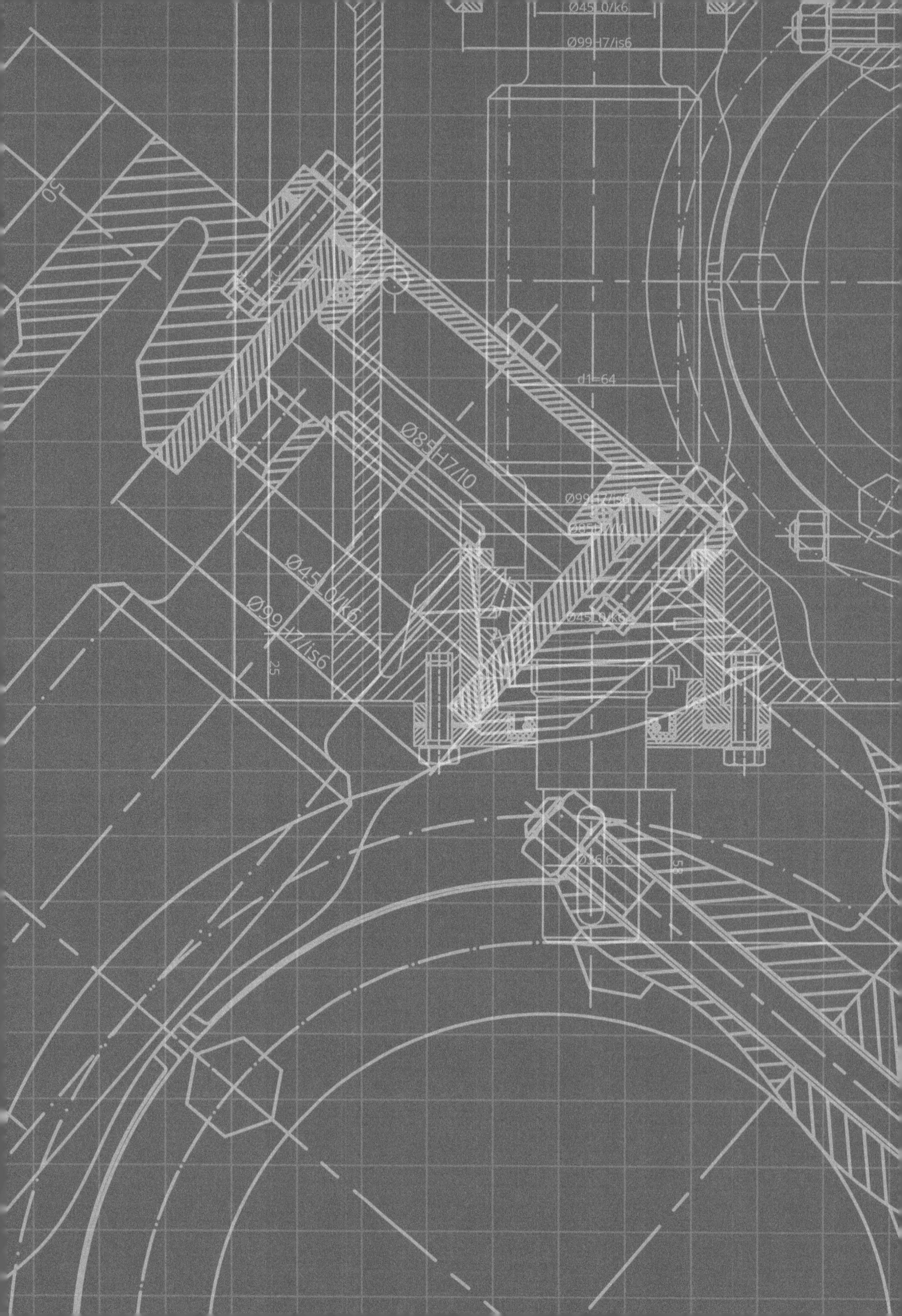

## CHAPTER 9
# Your Tax Pot

## HOW MUCH TO SET ASIDE — AND WHEN TO PAY IT

Tax bills hit hard — not because you didn't earn enough, but because no one told you how much to put aside, when to pay it, or how it even works.

Let's fix that.

Whether you're a sole trader or a limited company director, this chapter shows you:
- What taxes apply to you
- How to budget properly (without guesswork)
- When you need to actually pay the tax

## SOLE TRADER? HERE'S WHAT YOU PAY

### 1. Income Tax (England, Wales, NI)
- £12,570 tax-free (your personal allowance)
- 20% tax on income between £12,571–£50,270
- 40% £50,271-£125,140
- 45% if you go above that

You're taxed on **profit**, not total income.

### Income Tax (Scotland)
- £12,570 tax-free (your personal allowance)
- 19% tax on income between £12,571–£15,397
- 20% tax on income between £15,398-£27,491
- 21% tax on income between £27,492-£43,662
- 42% tax on income between £43,663-£75,000
- 45% tax on income between £75,001-£125,140
- 48% if you go above that

You're taxed on **profit**, not total income.

### 2. National Insurance (NI)
You'll pay:
- Class 2 NI (flat £179.40 per year if you earn over £6,725)
- Class 4 NI — 6% on profits between £12,570–£50,270

NI can feel like a "surprise tax" if you're not ready for it.

### 3. Payments on Account
This is the sneaky one.

If your tax bill is over £1,000, HMRC expects you to start paying next year's tax in advance.

How it works:
- You pay your full bill for the current year
- PLUS 50% of that bill towards next year
- Then 50% again six months later

This first time you get hit with it, it feels brutal — but from then on, you're always just topping up.

**WHAT TO SET ASIDE (SOLE TRADERS)**
Safe estimate:
Set aside 25%–30% of your profit as a general rule.

Break it down like this:

| PROFIT BAND | WHAT TO SET ASIDE |
|---|---|
| Up to £20,000 | ~20–25% |
| £20,000–£50,000 | ~25–30% |
| £50,000+ | ~30–35% (inc. higher rate tax) |

Better to over-save and have a bonus pot than under-save and panic.

## LIMITED COMPANY? HERE'S WHAT YOU PAY

### 1. Corporation Tax
- 19% on your profits (small companies rate — up to £50k profit)

### 2. Income Tax on Dividends
- First £500 tax-free
- Then 8.75% on the next chunk (basic rate)
- Higher if you earn more

### 3. PAYE/National Insurance
If you pay yourself a salary, the company pays Employer's NI, and you may pay some Employee NI (depending on the level).

## WHAT TO SET ASIDE (LTD COMPANIES)
Your company should set aside:
- 19% of profit for Corporation Tax
- Personal dividend tax — based on your overall income

If you're withdrawing money via salary and dividends, speak to your accountant to figure out:
- What tax you'll owe personally
- What tax the business will owe

You might need two pots:
1. Corp Tax Pot — for the company's liability
2. Personal Tax Pot — for dividend tax due via your Self Assessment

## WHEN DO YOU PAY TAX?

| TAX TYPE | DUE DATE |
|---|---|
| Self Assessment (sole traders/directors) | 31st January each year |
| Payments on Account | 31st Jan + 31st July |
| Corporation Tax | 9 months after year-end |
| PAYE (if on payroll) | 22nd of each month (or quarterly) |

### Set Up a Separate "Tax Pot" Account
Here's the game-changer:
- Open a separate business savings account
- Each month, transfer a % of profit or turnover into it
- Treat it like a non-negotiable expense

That way:
- You always have money ready for tax
- No scrambling in January
- Any extra left = a bonus

## REAL-LIFE EXAMPLE (SOLE TRADER)

You earn £3,000/month and spend £1,000/month on materials, fuel, etc.

That's £2,000/month profit.

Set aside 25% = £500/month ⇒ by January, you've saved £6,000 for tax.

Boom. No panic. No overdraft.

## BOTTOM LINE

Tax doesn't have to be terrifying — if you plan ahead.

> **Know your numbers**
> **Save little and often**
> **Use software to keep on top of it**

You'll go from dreading the taxman to feeling totally in control.

# Make It Yours

## Make It Yours

## Make It Yours

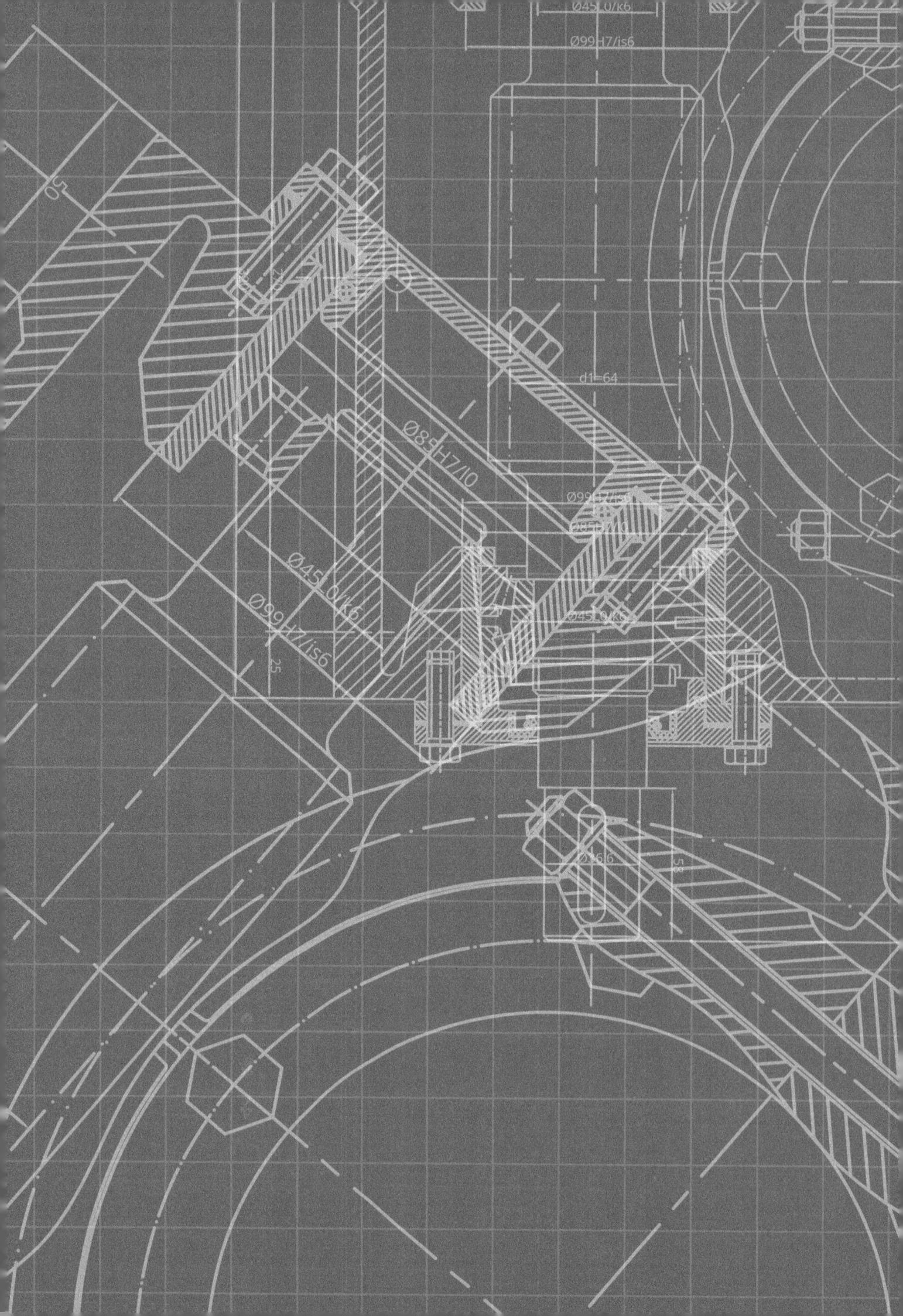

## CHAPTER 10
# How to Make Bookkeeping *Way Easier*

*(Even if you've got zero spare time and hate admin)*

Bookkeeping might not be your favourite part of running a business — but it's the part that can make or break how confident and in control you feel.

Good bookkeeping = clear profits, less stress, smaller tax bills, and better business decisions.

This chapter shows you how to:
- Take the hassle out of bookkeeping
- Avoid the most common mistakes
- Build easy habits that don't take over your week

## WHAT ACTUALLY IS BOOKKEEPING?

In plain English, bookkeeping is:

Keeping track of every penny that goes in or out of your business.

That includes:
- Recording income (invoices, job payments)
- Tracking expenses (tools, fuel, subs)
- Matching payments with your bank
- Saving receipts and proof of purchase

It doesn't mean spreadsheets with 20 tabs.

It means having a system you can stick to — ideally without wanting to throw your laptop out the window.

## WHY IT NEEDS TO BE REGULAR

The longer you leave it, the harder it gets.

If you:
- Only look at your accounts at tax time
- Stuff receipts into a shoebox
- Forget what payments were actually for

…you're making it harder than it needs to be — and risking missed claims, incorrect figures, or penalties.

**Little and often is the goal — 15 minutes a week is better than 4 hours in January.**

## TOOLS THAT MAKE IT 100X EASIER

### 1. ACCOUNTING SOFTWARE
Use something like:
- Xero
- FreeAgent
- QuickBooks
- Sage

What it does:
- Connects to your bank
- Lets you snap receipts from your phone
- Keeps everything HMRC-compliant
- Helps you see profit, not just cash flow

You don't need to be a numbers person — just a "log in once a week" person.

### 2. RECEIPT APPS
Use apps like:
- Dext
- AutoEntry
- Or just your accounting software's mobile app

Snap receipts as soon as you get them, or at the end of the day. Done.

### 3. SEPARATE BANK ACCOUNT
Always.

No more scrolling through your personal bank feed wondering if that McDonald's was a client lunch or not.

## BOOKKEEPING HABITS THAT ACTUALLY WORK

Here's what I recommend to clients who hate paperwork:

| HABIT | HOW OFTEN | TIME IT TAKES |
|---|---|---|
| Check your bank feed | Weekly | 10 mins |
| Reconcile transactions in Xero | Weekly | 10–15 mins |
| Snap/upload receipts | As you spend | 10 secs |
| Review unpaid invoices | Fortnightly | 5 mins |
| Set a "Money Monday" reminder | Weekly | 15 mins total |

Set a recurring calendar reminder. Stick the kettle on. You'll be done before your tea cools.

## COMMON BOOKKEEPING MISTAKES

- Mixing personal & business expenses
- Forgetting to record cash payments
- Not keeping proof of purchase
- Guessing instead of checking
- Doing it all once a year

### Bonus: Hire a Bookkeeper (if you can)

Even if you do most of it yourself, having a pro check your records regularly:
- Saves you time
- Helps you claim everything you're entitled to
- Avoids errors that can lead to fines or overpaid tax

You don't need to hand over everything — just the bits you hate or can't keep up with.

## BOTTOM LINE

Bookkeeping is just about building tiny habits and having the right tools.
- Start simple
- Keep things separate
- Do it often, not perfectly
- Don't be afraid to get help

## Make It Yours

# Make It Yours

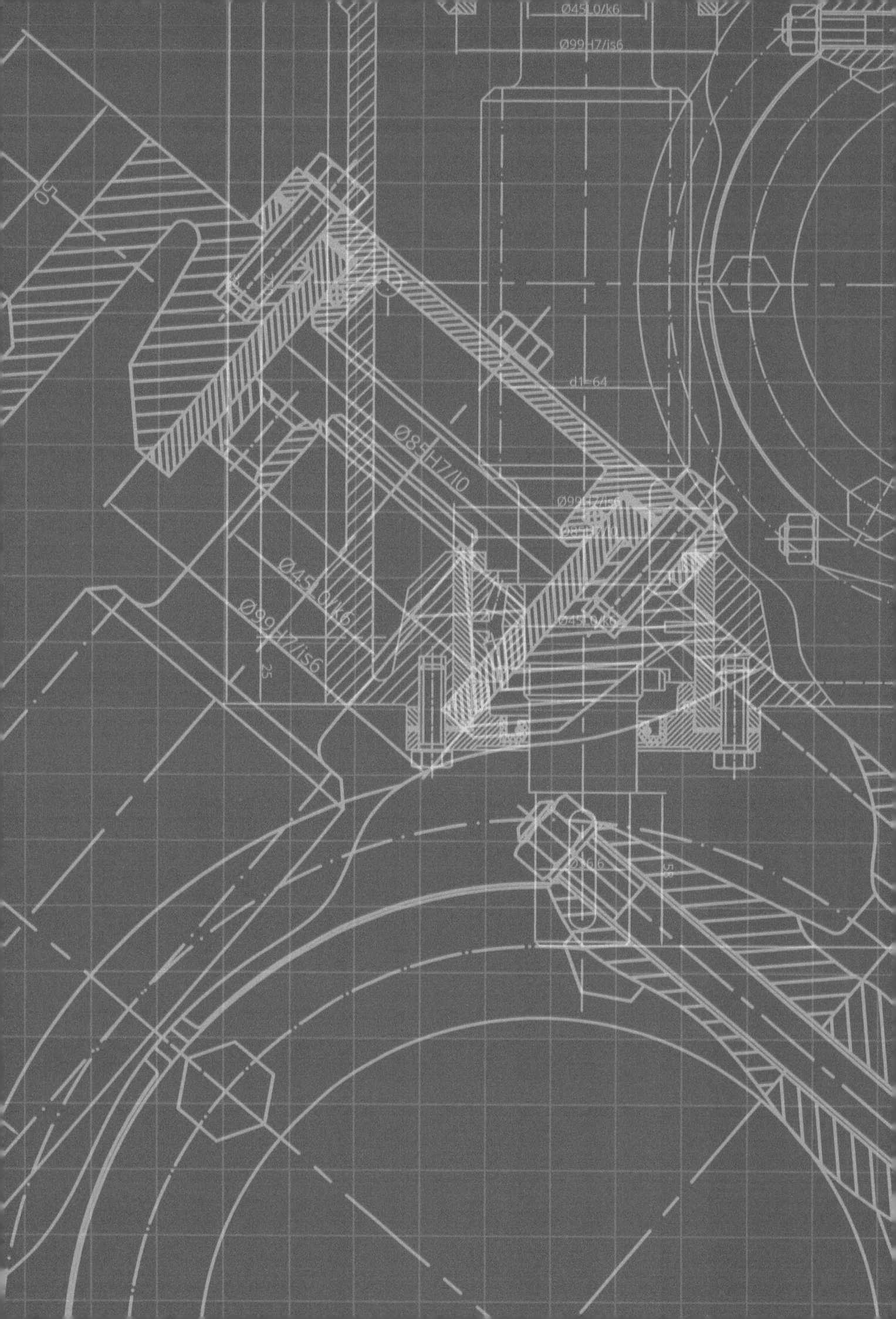

# CHAPTER 11
# Claiming Expenses Without Guesswork

*What you can claim, what you can't — and how to keep HMRC happy.*

You run a business. You spend money to make money.

So naturally, you want to claim back as much as possible.

But HMRC has rules — and there's a fine line between:
- Legit business costs
- Stuff you think should be claimable, but isn't
- Things that need extra care

This chapter gives you:
- A clear list of what's usually claimable
- Tips on how to prove it
- The no-go zones that trigger problems

## THE GOLDEN RULE

**Is it wholly and exclusively for the business?**

If the answer is YES — it's probably claimable.

If it's personal or a mix of both — it gets trickier.

HMRC looks at:
- Why you bought it
- Who used it
- Whether it has a personal benefit

# COMMON EXPENSES YOU CAN CLAIM

These are things most self-employed people or limited companies can claim (as long as they're business-related):

| TYPE OF EXPENSE | EXAMPLES |
| --- | --- |
| Tools & Equipment | Drills, laptops, diagnostic kits, software |
| Materials | Timber, paint, parts, stock |
| Protective Clothing | Steel toe boots, hi-vis, branded workwear |
| Fuel & Mileage | Business journeys, site visits |
| Vehicle Costs | Insurance, servicing, road tax (if business use) |
| Advertising & Marketing | Facebook ads, flyers, web hosting |
| Phones & Internet | Business portion only |
| Training | Courses that relate to your trade/business |
| Accountancy Fees | Yes — even this book counts |
| Bank Charges | Business account fees, card reader subscriptions |
| Subscriptions | Trade bodies, Xero, job boards |

## MIXED-USE ITEMS

Some things are partly for business and partly personal — like your phone, van, or home internet.

You can still claim, but you must:
- Be reasonable with the percentage
- Keep a record of how you worked it out
- Only claim the business portion

Example:
You use your mobile 70% for work — you can claim 70% of the bill.

## WHAT IF YOU WORK FROM HOME?

Yes — you can claim a portion of your home costs.

Two options:

### 1. Flat rate (easiest)

HMRC lets you claim a set amount per month based on how many hours you work from home:

| HOURS/MONTH | FLAT RATE |
| --- | --- |
| 25–50 hrs | £10 |
| 51–100 hrs | £18 |
| 101+ hrs | £26 |

No receipts needed.

### 2. Proportional method

If you want to claim a portion of rent, utilities, broadband etc:
- Divide total bills by number of rooms and % of business use
- Keep a spreadsheet as backup

Example:
- You use 1 of 5 rooms for 40 hours/week = 20% of the space.
- Claim 20% of heating/electric/broadband etc.

## CLAIMING FOR YOUR VEHICLE
There are two ways to claim car/van costs:

### 1. Mileage Method (simplest)
- Track your business miles
- Claim 45p/mile for the first 10,000 miles, then 25p/mile

This includes fuel, wear & tear, insurance etc — so you can't claim anything else.

### 2. Actual Cost Method
- Claim fuel, tax, insurance, servicing based on business use %
- Keep mileage logs to prove it

Vans used purely for business? You may be able to claim everything — check with your accountant.

## THINGS YOU CAN'T CLAIM (SORRY!)
Some things feel "sort of" business-related — but HMRC says no:

| NOT CLAIMABLE | WHY NOT |
| --- | --- |
| Daily lunch | It's a personal living cost |
| Clothes (non-branded) | Unless it's a uniform or PPE |
| Parking fines/speeding | HMRC won't reward breaking the law |
| Client entertainment | Food/drinks for clients — not allowed (mostly) |
| Gym membership | Even if it helps you de-stress — it's personal |

*"It's good for my business mindset" doesn't count with HMRC.*

# HOW TO KEEP PROOF (WITHOUT A SHOEBOX)

To claim expenses, you need evidence. That means:
- Receipts/invoices
- Bank transactions
- Notes on what it was for

Tips:
- Snap receipts as you get them (use apps like Xero, Dext or QuickBooks)
- Don't use cash unless you have a receipt
- Keep digital records for at least 6 years

# RULE OF THUMB

If you're not sure whether you can claim it — record it anyway and ask your accountant later.

It's better to have more info than not enough.

## BOTTOM LINE

You should claim everything you're entitled to — just don't get carried away.
- Know the rules
- Keep receipts
- Be reasonable with mixed-use stuff
- Track it as you go

This is where the real savings stack up — especially over years.

# Make It Yours

## Make It Yours

# Make It Yours

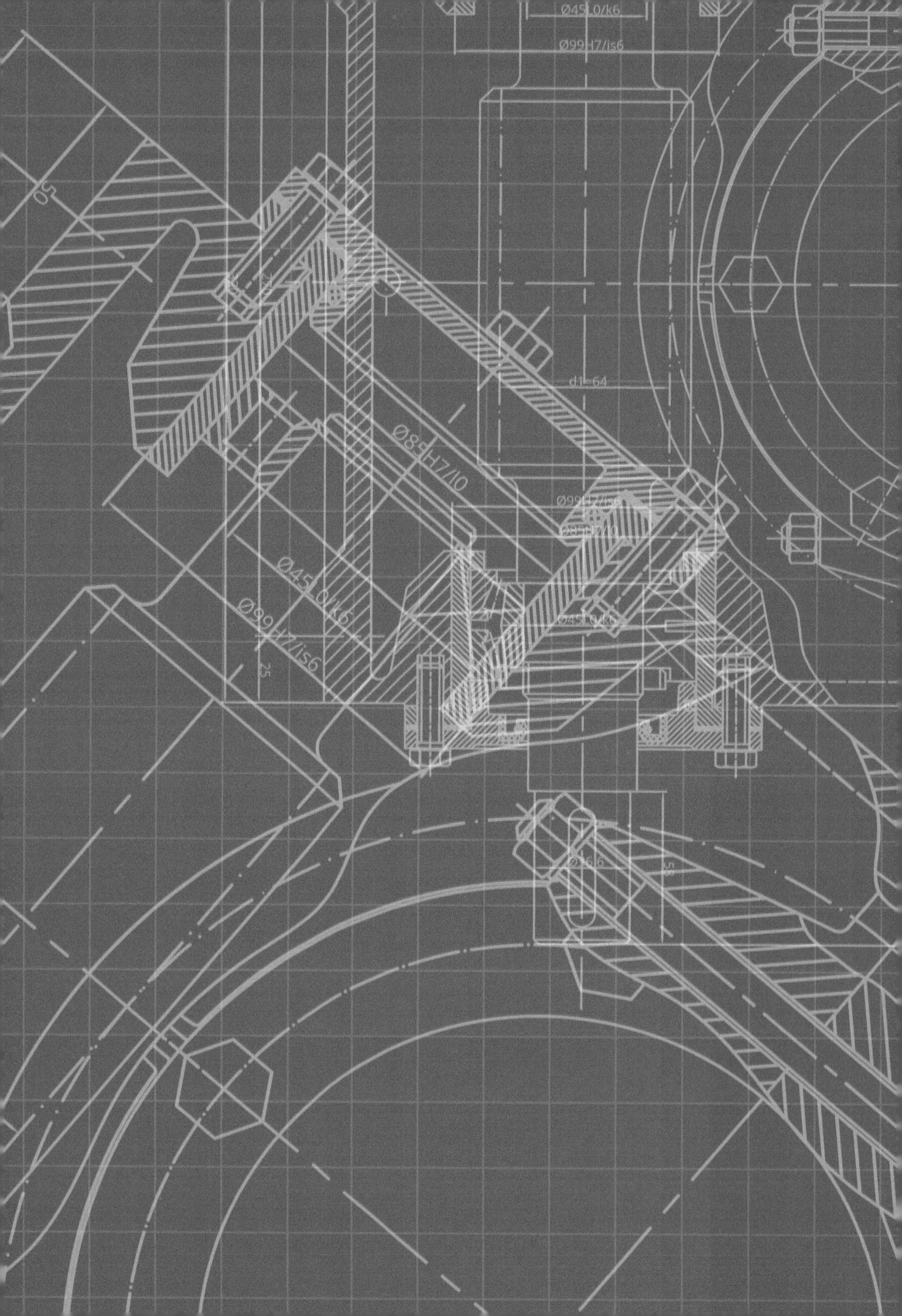

## CHAPTER 12
# The Final Checklist

## WHAT TO DO EACH MONTH, QUARTER & YEAR TO STAY ON TRACK

You've got the knowledge now.

The last piece is knowing when to do what, so it all stays easy, manageable, and stress-free.

This chapter gives you:
- A clear monthly/quarterly/yearly checklist
- A few habits to keep you consistent
- The peace of mind that nothing's getting missed

Let's go.

## YOUR MONTHLY BOOKKEEPING CHECKLIST

| TASK | WHY IT MATTERS |
| --- | --- |
| Download/snap all receipts | You need proof for every expense |
| Reconcile bank transactions | Keeps your books tidy and accurate |
| Review income vs. expenses | Know if you're making money (not just busy) |
| Set aside money for tax | No surprises come January or July |
| Chase unpaid invoices (if any) | You did the work — make sure you're paid |
| Back up your data | If your phone or laptop dies, you're safe |

Set a recurring reminder in your phone or calendar — even just 1 hour a month can do the trick.

## QUARTERLY CHECKLIST

(Especially if you're VAT registered or using software like Xero)

| TASK | TIP |
|---|---|
| Submit VAT return (if applicable) | Due 1 month + 7 days after quarter end |
| Review profit + cash flow | Are you actually making a profit? |
| Check any changes in business costs | Cancel unused subs or spot price hikes |
| Send records to your bookkeeper/accountant | Make their job easier, save yourself stress |

A quick Zoom with your accountant each quarter can make a massive difference to your clarity and confidence.

## YEAR-END CHECKLIST (SELF ASSESSMENT OR LTD COMPANY)

| TASK | WHEN TO DO IT |
|---|---|
| Pull together all income & expenses | After 5th April (Self Assessment) or your company year end |
| Submit Self Assessment tax return | Deadline: 31 Jan |
| Pay your tax bill | Deadline: 31 Jan (and July if POA applies) |
| Check if payments on account apply | You'll be told on your return summary |
| Review your pricing & income goals | Did you charge enough this year? |

If you have a bookkeeper/accountant, you'll just need to:
- Keep your records tidy
- Send them what they ask for
- Respond to queries quickly

That alone will save you SO much hassle.

## TIPS TO BUILD A ROUTINE THAT STICKS

1. **Pick a regular bookkeeping day** - (e.g. "Money Mondays" or the first Friday of each month)
2. **Keep receipts organised** - App > snap > bin it. Done.
3. **Automate what you can**

- Link your bank to Xero or QuickBooks
- Set reminders for VAT returns or tax deadlines

4. **Check in with your accountant** - They're not just for tax — they can help you grow the business too.
5. **Celebrate staying on track!** - You're building a better, less stressful business — give yourself credit for that.

## FINAL THOUGHTS FROM REBEKAH

You don't have to love numbers.

You just have to:
- Stay organised
- Use the right tools
- Ask for help when you need it

This guide wasn't about turning you into an accountant — it was about giving you control.

Because when you understand your numbers, you make better decisions.
You feel more confident.

And you stop fearing the taxman and start feeling like a proper business owner.

## WHAT'S NEXT?

If this guide helped you:
- Let's keep the momentum going!
- Book a free chat with me to see how I can help with your books, tax, or systems

# Let's build a business you're proud of — *without the bullsh*t.*

## Make It Yours

# Make It Yours

## Make It Yours

# Make It Yours

## Make It Yours

## Make It Yours

## Make It Yours

## Make It Yours

## Make It Yours

## Make It Yours

## Make It Yours

## Make It Yours

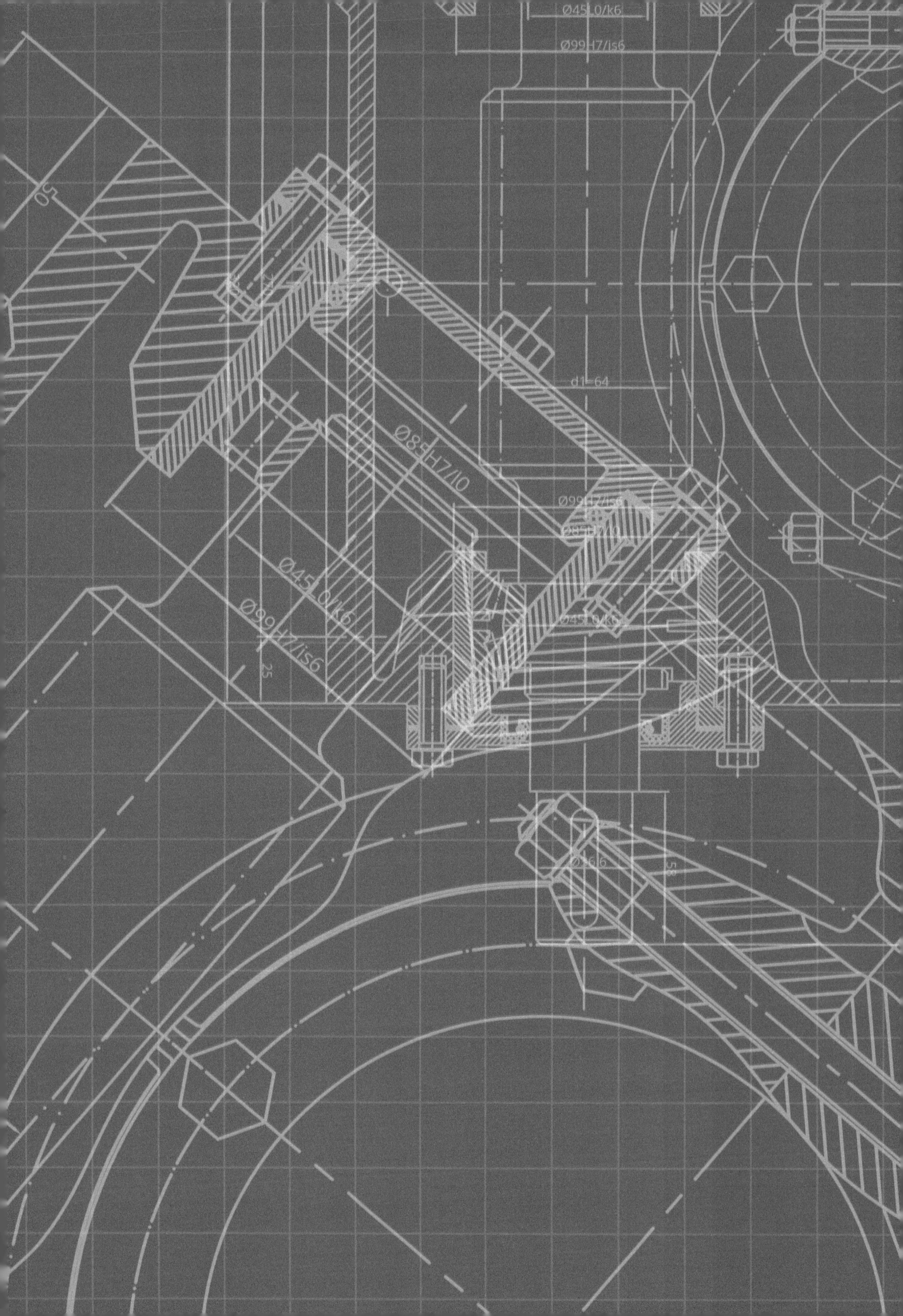

www.ingramcontent.com/pod-product-compliance
Lightning Source LLC
Chambersburg PA
CBHW061410070526
44584CB00032B/4201